Your Name, Your Tartan

CLANS, FAMILIES AND KINSFOLK

NO MATTER OUR STATION IN LIFE, we all have a surname – but it was not until the middle of the fourteenth century that the practice of being identified by a particular one became commonly established throughout the British Isles.

Previous to this, it was normal for a person to be identified through the use of only a forename, but as population gradually increased and there were many more people with the same forename, surnames were adopted to distinguish one person from another.

Many common surnames are patronymic in origin, meaning they stem from the forename of one's father – with 'Adamson', for example, indicating 'son of Adam'.

A unique feature of many Scottish surnames is the prefix 'Mac' and its abbreviated form of 'Mc' – Gaelic terms also indicating 'son of' – with MacGregor, for example, denoting 'son of Gregor' or 'son of Griogar'.

This Mac/Mc prefix is found in the names of the many clans originally found in the Highlands and

Islands, with 'clan' derived from the Gaelic *clanna*, meaning 'children.'

A clan, essentially, was a close-knit tribal grouping settled in a particular territory and whose members – or 'children', or 'kin' – owed unswerving loyalty to a chief who, in turn, was bound by duty and honour to protect them.

Not all members of a clan necessarily shared the same surname as the chief – known as *ceann-cinnidh*, meaning 'head and chief of the family' – and these 'kindred of the clan', or 'kinsfolk', were recognised, as they are to this day, as septs, or sub-branches of the clan.

As such, they are entitled to share in the clan's heritage and traditions that include the right to display its tartan and heraldry of crest and motto – this heraldry recognised by the Lord Lyon King of Arms of Scotland, the final arbiter on all matters heraldic.

In some cases, bearers of a particular surname are recognised as septs of more than one clan, because the name was not necessarily originally confined to only one territory.

Bearers of the Black name, for example, are recognised as septs of Clan Maclean of Duart, Clan Lamont and Clan MacGregor.

In the Lowlands, 'families', rather than clans predominated – the proud Borders clan of Clan Douglas

YOUR NAME - YOUR TARTAN

A guide to clan and family links and your tartan

by **Iain Gray**

INTRODUCTION

IN 2009, HOLYROOD PARK in Edinburgh was the venue for the two-day colourful extravaganza *The Gathering*.

A major feature of Scotland's Homecoming events, it saw proud representatives of more than 125 clans, including descendants of Scots who had forged new lives for themselves in foreign parts, join together in celebration of the nation's history and culture.

This also impressively included a Highland games and a glittering parade of swirling kilts and skirling bagpipes from Holyrood Palace to the Castle Esplanade.

What the events highlighted were traditions based on an ancient past that have survived to the present day – a heritage that we can connect to through clan links to the very surname we bear.

Presented here is a list of many of the most common surnames found in Scotland, their clan or family affiliations and the tartan that bearers of the name are entitled to proudly display, in addition to outlines on the origins of surnames and clans, how to choose your tartan and how to trace your family tree.

being one of the several exceptions – but they have the same recognised kinsfolk structure as the clans.

Not all clans today have a chief, while those that may have had one in the past are known as armigerous clans.

In 2018, a chief of Clan Buchanan – John Michael Baillie-Hamilton Buchanan and known by his title of 'The Buchanan' – was finally recognised by the Lord Lyon King of Arms following many years of intensive genealogical research, the title having fallen into abeyance in 1681 following the death without male heirs of the last chief.

The origins of many clans are steeped in romantic myth and legend.

Taking the MacGregors, more properly known as Clan Gregor, as an example, they claim a descent from Gregor, or Griogar, a son of Alpin who was a king of ancient Dalriada – explaining the proud clan motto of 'Royal is my race', while the MacDonalds are said to descend from Donald, a grandson of the 12th century warrior of the Western Isles, Somerled.

The origins of other clans can be more readily traced.

The Sinclairs, for example, of original Norse blood, take their name from St Clair, in Normandy. Fighting at the side of William the Conqueror at the battle of Hastings in 1066, they were subsequently granted lands in Scotland during the reign from 1124 to 1153 of King David I.

Other sources of clan or family names relate to the name of the area in which they were settled.

The Urquharts, for example, derive their name from the territory known in Gaelic as *Urchard*, or *Airchartdan*, on the shores of Loch Ness.

Linguistic roots of surnames that came into usage throughout the British Isles include not only Norman-French and Gaelic but also Old French, Old Norse, Old English, Middle English, German, Latin, Greek and Hebrew.

Many of these names were coined in connection with occupation, such as Baker and Smith, while Cooks and Clarks were to be found carrying out duties on royal estates and large medieval households.

Even the scenery was utilised, as in Forest, Hill, Moor and Wood, while the hunt and the chase supplied names that include Fox and Hunter.

Colours are also a source of surnames, such as Black, Brown, Gray, Green and White, and would originally have denoted the colour of clothing a person habitually wore or, apart from the obvious exception of Green, their hair colour or complexion.

Echoes of a far distant past can still be found in our surnames, and they can be borne with pride in commemoration of our forebears.

ROOTS TO BRANCHES
– Tracing Your Family Tree

IF YOU DON'T KNOW WHERE you come from, you won't know where you're going **is a frequently quoted observation and one that has a particular resonance today, when there has been a marked upsurge in interest in genealogy, with increasing numbers of people curious to trace their family roots.**

Main sources for genealogical research include official records, and the key to unlocking the detail they contain is obviously a family surname, one that has been 'inherited' and passed from generation to generation.

While a number of private enterprises offer, for a fee, in-depth genealogical research on your behalf, one excellent resource for names with a Scottish connection is provided through **ScotlandsPeople (www.Scotlandspeople.gov.uk)**

– an exclusive partnership between the Court of the Lord Lyon King of Arms and the National Records of Scotland.

Launched in 2008 and with its headquarters at 2 Princes Street, Edinburgh, this official Scottish government resource offers a wealth of information on family history.

While its indexes can be consulted free of charge, digital images you find in the indexes can be accessed on a 'pay-for-view' basis, while the headquarters also provides a dedicated 'search room'.

It is thanks to the meticulous recording over the centuries that details of key moments in the human experience such as births, marriages and deaths have been recorded.

These are all held in the **Statutory Registers**, and are collated from original sources including **Old Parish Registers (OPRs)** of **births**, **baptisms**, **marriage banns**, **deaths** and **burials** recorded by parishes of the Church of Scotland before what is known as civil registration (also recorded) in 1855.

Roman Catholic Registers also provide valuable information that includes **communicants** and **converts**.

Providing what ScotlandsPeople describes as 'a snapshot of the people at a particular address on a given night', **Census Returns** have been carried out every ten years since 1841.

On the year in question, the information provided by the householder was as at midnight on, for example,

June 6, 1841, March 30, 1851, April 3, 1881 and April 2, 1911.

In addition to providing the names and ages of all residents of a particular address, the returns also record occupations, where applicable.

Closed to public scrutiny for 100 years, it will not be until January of 2022 that the census of June 19, 1921, will be released.

Wills and testaments are also a source of background information – with the will the document drawn up by someone in order to settle their affairs before they die, and the testament the document drawn up after death to enable an executor to wind up the deceased's affairs.

But before embarking on a search of the Statutory Registers in order to trace your roots, it is worthwhile as a starting point to attempt to source and examine, if available, old **family correspondence** such as letters and even postcards and again – if available – family Bibles that record births, baptisms, marriages and deaths.

Oral testimonies, from the lips of family members, particularly the elderly, can also be mined for treasures they may contain – affording a snapshot of the bygone lives and times of our forebears.

WHICH TARTAN?

IT WASN'T UNTIL 1822, following a celebrated tartan pageant masterminded by the antiquarian and author Sir Walter Scott for the visit of King George IV to Edinburgh, that clan names were 'assigned' tartans.

But obviously there was not going to be a tartan for every surname, so which tartan should be adopted for those for which none had been designed?

It became practice to take into consideration that most clans included, as noted earlier, septs or sub-branches who, despite bearing a different name from the chief and his blood relatives, nevertheless shared kinship with the clan.

As such, these septs are entitled to display its tartan.

Bearers of many family names meanwhile, as opposed to clan names, also have their own recognised tartan.

For those who do not have a recognised clan or family connection, it is acceptable to take your mother's surname and, if this does have a clan or family tartan, to wear that.

Should this prove fruitless, you can also resort to

other names from your family that may link to a particular tartan.

Another possibility is to adopt a 'district' tartan – such as Aberdeen District, Edinburgh District, Glasgow District, Nithsdale District or Perthshire District – that relates to where some of your forebears may have been originally settled.

The Scottish Tartans Authority (STA) notes: "If you know the name of the city or area, then try typing that into the 'Tartan Name' search box (on the STA website www.tartansauthority.com).

"If that doesn't come up with anything, then type 'District' into the keywords search box and read through the listings."

Other tartan connections may be found through looking at previous family occupations – those associated with the ecclesiastical realm, for example, and as noted by the STA, may choose to wear the Priest or Clergy tartan.

In the military sphere, there are also a number of regimental tartans, while today increasing numbers of clubs, institutions, societies, colleges and universities have their own proud tartan.

An American tartan designed by James D. Scarlett of Milton of Moy, Inverness-shire, first came out during the American Bicentennial celebrations in 1976.

Originally known as the American Bicentennial

tartan, it is now known as American Saint Andrews – having been first adopted by the St Andrew's Society of Washington, DC.

It was designed for the special purpose of having a tartan for Americans who have no particular reason for wearing any of the clan tartans, in addition to providing a choice for a second kilt for any American – while there are also tartans for all of the Canadian provinces, and Maple Leaf with a white dress variant for general use by Canadians.

Personal tartans are those designed for the sole use of the owner, the STA points out, and can't be worn by anyone of the same name unless they have the owner's permission.

'Name tartans', meanwhile, allow anyone of the same name to wear them – the owner having granted permission to do so.

A major step in the evolution of tartans has been the growth in popularity of 'universal', 'general', or 'free' tartans, while the STA notes that among the most popular are the Jacobite, Royal Stewart (as worn by the Queen), Hunting Stewart and Black Watch.

Also known as Grant Hunting, Old Campbell and Government, Black Watch is also the tartan of a number of military bands throughout the British Commonwealth.

More contemporary tartans include a range of 'Pride of Scotland' tartans that include Pride of Scotland Dark,

Pride of Scotland Dress (Dance), Pride of Scotland Gold and Pride of Scotland Silver.

Not solely confined to fabric, tartan is also found in an eclectic variety of products that range from tea towels and scarves to carpets, curtains and coasters, while it was during the Victorian era that a voracious fad for 'tartan-ware' items such as jewellery boxes, snuff boxes and table-ware was born.

Through all its colourful range of colours, designs and products, tartan remains proudly iconic of Scotland.

Name	Clan(s)/Family & Tartan
Alexander	MacAlister, MacDonell of Glengarry, MacDonald of Clanranald, MacFarlane
Allan/Allen	MacDonald of Clanranald, MacFarlane
Allason	Grant, MacDonald, MacFarlane, Macpherson
Alison/Allison	Grant, MacAlister, MacDonald, MacFarlane, Allison
Allardice/Allardyce Graham	
Anderson	Ross, Anderson
Andrew	As above
Angus	MacInnes
Arbuthnot	Arbuthnot
Archibald	Macpherson
Armstrong	Armstrong
Arrol	Arrol
Arthur	MacArthur

Name	Clan(s)/Family & Tartan
Atholl	Murray of Atholl, Stewart of Atholl, Robertson
Atkin/Atkins	Gordon
Auld	Pertshire District
Austin	Keith, Austin
Ayson	Mackintosh of Glentit
Bain	Mackay
Baird	Baird
Bailey/Baillie	Baillie
Baird	Baird
Balfour	Balfour
Ballantyne	Campbell of Argyll
Bannatyne	Campbell of Argyll
Bannerman	Forbes
Barber/Barbour Montgomery	
Barclay	Barclay
Bartholomew	MacFarlane
Baxter	MacMillan
Bayne	Mackay

NAMES, CLANS AND TARTANS

COMMON NAMES with Scottish roots are alphabetically arranged in the first column, while the second lists the corresponding clan or family affiliations and the tartan, or tartans, associated with the name. With the prefix 'Mc' simply an abbreviation of 'Mac', the latter prefix is adopted throughout. As you will see there can of course be more than one clan or tartan associated with a name. In recent times more tartans have been created to match names and these compliment the older tartans linked to clans.

Name	Clan(s)/Family & Tartan	Name	Clan(s)/ Family & Tartan
Abercrombie	Abercrombie	Adamson	Gordon, Mackintosh
Abernethy/		Addison	Gordon
Abernethy	Fraser, Leslie	Adie	Gordon
Abbot	Macnab	Agnew	Agnew, Douglas
Abbotson	As above	Airlie	Ogilvie
Acheson	Gordon	Atchison	Gordon
Adair	Maxwell	Aitken	Gordon
Adam	Gordon		

Names, Clans and Tartans

Name	Clan(s)/Family & Tartan
Carruthers	Bruce
Caw	MacFarlane
Chalmers	Cameron
Chambers	Cameron
Cheyne	Sutherland
Chisholm	Chisholm
Christie	Farquharson
Clark/Clarke	Cameron, Mackintosh, Macpherson, Clark
Clarkson	As above
Clement	Lamont
Clerk	As above
Clyne	Sinclair
Cochran (e)	Clan Donald North, Clan Donald South, Cochrane (e)
Cockburn	Cockburn
Collier	Robertson
Colman	Buchanan
Colquhoun	Colquhoun

Name	Clan(s)/Family & Tartan
Colson	MacDonald (Clan Donald, North and South)
Combie	Mackintosh
Comrie	MacGregor or MacGrigor
Comyn	Cumin
Connall/Connell	MacDonald (Clan Donald, North and South)
Conochie	Campbell of Inverawe
Cook	Stewart of Appin
Cooper	Cooper
Cormack	Buchanan
Coulson	MacDonald (Clan Donald, North and South)
Coutts	Farquharson
Cowan (en)	Colquhoun, MacDougall
Cranston	Cranston
Craig	Gordon, Craig
Crauford/Craufurd	Crawford
Crawford	Crawford

Your Name, Your Tartan

Name	Clan(s)/Family & Tartan
Bean	MacBean
Beath	MacDonald (Clan Donald, North and South), Maclean of Duart
Beaton	MacDonald (Clan Donald, North and South), Maclean of Duart, Macleod of Harris
Begg	Drummond
Bell	Macmillan
Berkeley	Barclay
Bethune	MacDonald (Clan Donald, North and South), Macleod of Harris
Beton	As above
Bisset/Bissett	Fraser, Grant
Black	Lamont, MacGregor, Maclean of Duart
Blackie	Lamont
Blair	Graham of Menteith, Blair
Bonar/Bonnar	Graham of Montrose
Borthwick	Borthwick

Name	Clan(s)/Family & Tartan
Bowman	Farquharson
Boyd	Stewart (Royal), Boyd
Brieve	Morrison
Brodie	Brodie
Brown	Lamont, Macmillan, Brown
Bruce	Bruce
Buchan	Cumin
Buchanan	Buchanan
Burdon	Lamont
Burns	Campbell of Argyll, Burns Check
Caddell	Campbell of Cawdor
Caird	Sinclair
Callandar (er)	MacGregor
Calder	Campbell of Cawdor
Callum	Macleod of Raasay
Cameron	Cameron
Cameron	Cameron
Campbell	Campbell
Campbell	Campbell
Carmichael	Stewart of Appin, Stewart of Galloway
Carr	Kerr

Names, Clans and Tartans

Name	Clan(s)/Family & Tartan
Downie	Lindsay
Drummond	Drummond
Drysdale	Douglas
Duff	MacDuff
Duffie/Duffy	Macfie
Dunbar	Dunbar
Duncan	Robertson, Duncan
Duncanson	As above
Dundas	Dundas
Dunnachie	Robertson
Dyce	Skene
Easton	Easton
Edie	Gordon
Elder	Mackintosh
Elliot	Elliot
Erskine	Erskine
Ewan/Ewen	MacLachlan
Ewing	As above
Fairbairn	Armstrong

Name	Clan(s)/Family & Tartan
Falconer	Keith
Farquhar	Farquharson
Farquharson	Farquharson
Fergusson/ Fergus/Fergie	Ferguson
Ferries	Farquharson
Fife	MacDuff
Finlay/Findlay	Farquharson
Findlayson	As above
Fisher	Campbell of Argyll
Fleming	Murray
Fletcher	MacGregor
Forbes	Forbes
Fordyce	As above
Forest	Douglas
Forrester	MacDonald, Forrester
Forsyth(e)	Forsyth
Foulis	Munro
France	Stewart (Royal)

Your Name, Your Tartan

Name	Clan(s)/Family & Tartan
Grerar	Mackintosh
Crookshanks	Stewart of Garth
Crosbie	Bruce
Crosier/Crozier	Armstrong
Cruickshanks	Stewart of Garth
Cumming	Cumin, Cumming
Cunningham (e)	Cunningham
Currie	MacDonald of Clanranald, Macpherson, Currie
Dallas	Mackintosh
Dalzell/Dalziel	Dalzell
Darroch	MacDonald (Clan Donald, North and South)
Davidson	Davidson
Davie	As above
Davis	As above
Davison	As above
Dickson	Keith, Dickson
Dawson	As above

Name	Clan(s)/Family & Tartan
Deuchar	Lindsay
Dewar	Menzies, Macnab
Dickson	Keith
Dingwall	Munro, Ross
Dobson	Robertson
Docharty/ Docherty	MacGregor
Donachie	Robertson
Donald	MacDonald (Clan Donald, North and South)
Donaldson	As above
Donleavy	Buchanan
Dougall	MacDougall
Douglas	Douglas
Dove	Buchanan
Dow	Buchanan, Davidson
Dowall	MacDougall
Dowe	Buchanan
Dowell	MacDougall

Name	Clan(s)/Family & Tartan
Gunn	Gunn
Haig	Haig
Haliburton	Home
Hall	Skene, Hall
Hamilton	Hamilton
Hardie/Hardy	Farquharson, Mackintosh
Harper	Buchanan
Hawthorn	MacDonald (Clan Donald, North and South)
Hay	Hay
Henderson	Gunn, MacDonald of Glencoe, Henderson
Hendrie/Hendry	MacNaughton
Hewison	MacDonald (Clan Donald, North and South)
Hill	Hill
Home	Home
Hossack	Macintosh

Name	Clan(s)/Family & Tartan
Houston	MacDonald (Clan Donald, North and South)
Howison	As above
Hughes	Hughes
Hunter	Hunter of Bute, Hunter of Hunterston
Huntly	Gordon
Hutcheson	MacDonald (Clan Donald, North and South)
Hutchinson	As above
Hutchison	As above
Inches	Robertson
Inglis	Douglas
Ingram	Colquhoun
Innes	Macinnes
Irvine	Irvine
Isles	MacDonald (Clan Donald, North and South)

Your Name, Your Tartan

Name	Clan(s)/Family & Tartan
Fraser/Frazer	Fraser
Fullarton/ Fullerton	Stuart of Bute
Fyfe	MacDuff
Galbraith	MacDonald (Clan Donald, North and South), MacFarlane
Gallie	Gunn
Garrow	Stewart (Royal)
Geddes	Gordon, Rose, Scott, Geddes
Gibb/Gibson	Buchanan
Gibson	Buchanan
Gifford	Hay
Gilbert/ Gilberston	Buchan
Gilbride	MacDonald (Clan Donald, North and South)
Gilchrist	MacLachlan, Ogilvie
Gilfillan	Macnab
Gillanders	Ross

Name	Clan(s)/Family & Tartan
Gillespie	Macpherson
Gillies	Macpherson
Gilmore	Morrison
Gilroy	Grant of Glenmoriston, MacGillivray
Glen/Glennie	Mackintosh
Gordon	Gordon
Gow	Macpherson
Gowan	Clan Donald (North and South)
Gowrie	MacDonald (Clan Donald, North and South)
Graeme/Graham (e)	Graham of Menteith, Graham of Montrose
Grant	Grant
Gray	Stewart of Atholl, Sutherland, Gray
Gregor/Gregory	MacGregor
Greig	As above
Grier	As above
Grierson	As above
Grigor	As above

Name	Clan(s)/Family & Tartan	Name	Clan(s)/Family & Tartan
Law	MacLaren	Luke	Lamont
Lean	MacLean	Lyall/Lyel	Sinclair
Leckie	MacGregor	Lyon	Farquharson
Lecky	MacGregor	MacAdam	MacGregor
Lees	Macpherson	MacAdie	Ferguson
Lennie	Buchanan	MacAlaster	MacAlister
Lennox	MacFarlane, Stewart (Royal)	MacAlduie	Lamont
Leslie/Lesley	Leslie	MacAlester	MacAlister
Lewis	Macleod of Lewis	MacAlister	MacAlister
Limond	Lamont	MacAllan	MacDonald of Clanranald, As above
Lindsay	Lindsay	MacAllister	MacAlister
Livingston	Stewart of Appin	MacAlister	MacFarlane
Lobban	MacLennan	MacAlpin/	
Logan	As above	MacAlpine	MacAlpine
Lomond	Lamont	McAndrew	Mackintosh
Loudoun	Campbell of Loudoun	MacArthur	MacArthur
Love	Mackinnon	MacAskill	Macleod of Lewis
Low (e)	MacLaren	MacAulay	MacAulay
Lucas	Lamont	MacAuslan (d)	Buchanan

Your Name, Your Tartan

Name	Clan(s)/Family & Tartan
Jameson/ Jamieson	Gunn, Stuart of Bute
Jamieson	As above
Jardine	Jardine
Johnson	Gunn, MacDonald (MacIan), of Ardnamurchan, and of Glencoe
Johnston/ Johnstone	Johnstone
Johnstoun	As above
Jones	Jones
Kay	Davidson
Kean/Keene	Gunn, MacDonald (MacIan), of Ardnamurchan, and of Glencoe
Keith	Keith, Macpherson, Sutherland
Kellie	MacDonald (Clan Donald, North and South)
Kelly	As above
Kendrick	MacNaughton
Kennedy	Cameron, Kennedy

Name	Clan(s)/Family & Tartan
Kenneth	Mackenzie
Kerr	Kerr
Kilpatrick	Colquhoun
Kirkpatrick	Douglas
King	MacGregor
Kinnell	MacDonald
Kinnieson	MacFarlane
Kirkpatrick	Colquhoun
Lachlan	MacLachlan
Laidlaw	Scott
Laing	Colquhoun
Laird	Sinclair
Lamb/Lambie	Lamont
Lammie	As above
Lamond	As above
Lamondson	As above
Lamont	As above
Landers	As above
Lauder	Lauder

Name	Clan(s)/Family & Tartan	Name	Clan(s)/Family & Tartan
MacDowall (e)	MacDougall	MacGilroy	Grant of Glenmoriston, MacGillivray
MacDuff	MacDuff	MacGilvray	MacGillivray
MacDuffie	Macfie	MacGilp	MacDonnell of Keppoch
MacEacharan	MacDonald (Clan Donald, North and South)	MacGowan	MacDonald (Clan Donald, North and South), Macpherson
MacEwan/		MacGregor	MacGregor
MacEwen	MacEwan	MacGrory	MacLaren
Macfadyen	Maclaine of Lochbuie	Macgrowther	MacGregor
MacFall	Mackintosh	MacGuire	Macquarrie
MacFarlan(e)	MacFarlane	MacHay	Mackintosh, Shaw
MacFarquhar	Farquharson	MacHendry	MacNaughton
MacFater	MacLaren	MacHugh	MacDonald (Clan Donald, North and South)
Macfie/Macfee	Macfie		
MacGaw	MacFarlane	MacHutchen	As above
Macghee	Mackay	MacHutcheson	As above
Macghie	As above	MacIldowie	Cameron
MacGibbon	Buchanan of Sallochy, Campbell of Argyll, Graham of Menteith	Macilroy	MacGillivray, Grant of Glenmoriston
MacGillivray	MacGillivray	Macilvain	MacBean

Name	Clan(s)/Family & Tartan
MacAuslane	Buchanan
MacBain	MacBean
MacBeth	MacBean, MacDonald (Clan Donald, North and South), Maclean of Duart
MacBrayne	MacNaughton
MacBride	MacDonald (Clan Donald, North and South)
MacCaig	Farquharson, MacLeod of Harris
MacCall	MacDonald (Clan Donald, North and South)
MacCallum	MacCallum
MacCalman	Buchanan
MacCalmont	As above
MacCartney	Farquharson
MacCaskill	MacLeod of Lewis
MacCaw	MacFarlane, Stuart of Bute
MacClure	MacLeod of Harris
MacClymont	Lamont

Name	Clan(s)/Family & Tartan
MacColl	MacDonald (Clan Donald, North and South)
MacColman	Buchanan
MacCombe	Mackintosh
MacConachie	Robertson
MacConnechy	Campbell of Inverawe, Robertson
MacConnell	MacDonald (Clan Donald, North and South)
MacCormack	Buchanan
MacCormick	Maclaine of Lochbuie
MacCorry	Macquarrie
MacDermid	Campbell of Argyll
MacDiarmid	As above
MacDonald	MacDonald of Ardnamurchan, (Clan Donald) MacDonald of Clanranald, MacDonald of the Isles and of Sleat; MacDonell of Glengarry, MacDonell of Keppoch)
MacDougall	MacDougall

Name	Clan(s)/Family & Tartan
MacLauchlan	MacLachlan
MacLaughlan	MacLachlan
MacLaurin	MacLaren
MacLaverty	MacDonald (Clan Donald, North and South)
Maclay	Stewart of Appin
Maclean	Maclean, Maclean of Duart
MacLeish	Macpherson
MacLellan	MacLellan
Maclennan	Maclennan
MacLeod	MacLeod of Harris, MacLeod of Lewis
MacLewis	MacLeod of Lewis, Stuart of Bute
Maclymont	Lamont
MacMartin	Cameron
MacMaster	Buchanan, MacInnes
MacMenzies	Menzies
MacMichael	Stewart of Appin, Stewart of Galloway
Macmillan	Macmillan

Name	Clan(s)/Family & Tartan
MacMinn	Menzies
MacMurdo	MacDonald (Clan Donald, North and South), Macpherson
MacMurdoch	As above
MacMurray	Murray
MacMutrie	Stuart of Bute
Macnab	Macnab
MacNair	MacFarlane, MacNaughton
MacNaughton	MacNaughton
MacNeal	MacNeil of Barra, MacNeil of Gigha
MacNeill	As above
MacNeish	MacGregor
MacNichol	Campbell of Argyll
MacNicol	MacNicol
MacNeil of Gigha	MacNeil of Gigha
MacNish	MacGregor
MacOmish	Gunn
MacOwen	Campbell of Argyll

Name	Clan(s)/Family & Tartan	Name	Clan(s)/Family & Tartan
Macilwraith	MacDonald (Clan Donald, North and South)	MacKeith	Macpherson
Macimmey	Fraser	MacKellar	Campbell of Argyll
Macinally	Buchanan	MacKendrick	MacNaughton
Macindoe	As above	MacKenrick	MacNaughton
Macinnes	Macinnes	Mackenzie	Mackenzie
Macinroy	Robertson	MacKerracher	Farquharson
Macintosh	Mackintosh	Mackie	Mackay
Mackintosh	Mackintosh	MacKillop	MacDonell of Keppoch
Macintyre	Macintyre	Mackinlay(ey)	Buchanan
MacIsaac	Campbell of Craignish, MacDonald of Clanranald	Mackinney	Mackinnon
MacIver	Campbell of Argyll, Robertson of Struan, MacKenzie	Mackinning	As above
		Mackinnon	As above
MacIvor	As above	Mackintosh	Mackintosh
Mackay	Mackay	Macknight	MacNaughton
MacKean	Gunn, MacDonald of Ardnamurchan, MacDonald of Glencoe	MacLachlan	MacLachlan
		Maclae	Stewart of Appin
Mackechnie	MacDonald of Clanranald	Maclagan	Robertson
		MacLamond	Lamont
		MacLaren	MacLaren

Name	Clan(s)/Family & Tartan	Name	Clan(s)/Family & Tartan
Matheson	Matheson	More	Leslie
Maxwell	Maxwell	Morgan	Mackay
May	MacDonald (Clan Donald, North and South)	Morison	Morrison
		Morrison	Buchanan, Morrison
Meikle	Lamont	Morton	Douglas
Meikleham	Lamont	Mowat	Sutherland
Menteith	Graham, Stewart (Royal)	Muir	Gordon, Muir
Menzies	Menzies	Munro	Munro
Michie	Forbes	Murdoch	MacDonald (Clan Donald, North and South), Macpherson
Millar/Miller	MacFarlane		
Milligan	Galloway District	Murray of Atholl	Murray of Atholl, Murray of Tullibardine
Milne/Mylne	Gordon		
Mitchel	Mitchell	Napier	MacFarlane
Moffat	Moffat	Nairn(e)	MacIntosh
Moir	Gordon	Neal/Neil(l)	MacNeil
Monro(e)	Munro	Neilson	Mackay
Monteith	Graham, Stewart (Royal)	Neish	MacGregor
Montgomery	Montgomery	Nelson	Gunn
Moray	Murray	Nicholl(son)	MacLeod of Lewis, Nicolson

Your Name, Your Tartan

Name	Clan(s)/Family & Tartan
MacPhail	Cameron, Mackintosh, Mackay
Macphee (ie)	Macfie
Macpherson	Macpherson
MacPhilip	Macdonell of Keppoch
Macquarie	Macquarie
MacRae	MacRae
MacRankin	Maclean of Coll
Macritchie	Mackintosh
MacRob	Gunn, MacFarlane
MacRobert	Robertson
MacRorie	MacDonald (Clan Donald, North and South)
MacRory	As above, also MacLaren
MacSimon	Fraser
MacSorley	Cameron, MacDonald (Clan Donald, North and South)
MacSween	Macqueen
MacTaggart	Ross
MacTavish	MacTavish

Name	Clan(s)/Family & Tartan
MacTear	Ross, Macintyre
MacVey	Maclean of Duart
MacVicar	MacNaughton
MacVurrish	MacDonald of Clanranald, Macpherson
MacWalter	MacFarlane
MacWhirter	Buchanan
MacWilliam	Gunn, MacFarlane
Malcolm	Malcolm
Malcolmson	Macleod of Raasay
Manson	Gunn
Marshall	Marshall
Martin	Cameron, MacDonald (North and South)
Mason	Sinclair
Massie	Matheson
Masterson	Buchanan
Matheson	Matheson
Mathie	As above

Name	Clan(s)/Family & Tartan
Robison	Gunn
Robson	Gunn
Roderick	MacDonald
Ronald (son)	MacDonell of Keppoch
Rose	Rose
Ross	Ross
Roy	Robertson
Ruskin	MacCalman, Buchanan
Russell	Cumming, Russell
Ruthven	Ruthven
Sanderson	MacDonell of Glengarry
Sandison	Gunn
Scott	Scott
Shannon	MacDonald (Clan Donald, North and South)
Shaw	Mackintosh, Shaw
Sim (e)	Fraser
Simon	As above
Simpson	As above

Name	Clan(s)/Family & Tartan
Sinclair	Sinclair
Skene	Skene
Small	Murray
Smith/Smythe	MacFarlane, Macpherson, Smith
Sorley	Cameron, MacDonald (Clan Donald, North and South), Lamont
Spalding	Murray
Spence	MacDuff
Spens	As above
Stalker	MacFarlane
Stark	Robertson
Stevenson/	
Stephenson	Stevenson, Stephenson
Stewart/Stuart	Royal Stewart, Stewart of Appin, Stewart of Atholl, Stewart of Galloway, Stuart of Bute
Sutherland	Sutherland
Swan	Macqueen
Swanson	Gunn

Your Name, Your Tartan

Name	Clan(s)/Family & Tartan
Nicol	Macleod of Lewis, Nicolson
Nicolson	As above
Nish	MacGregor
Niven	Cumin, Mackintosh, MacNaughton
Nixon	Armstrong
Noble	Mackintosh
Norman	Macleod of Harris
Ogilvie/Ogilvy	Ogilvie
Oliphant	Sutherland
Oliver	Fraser
Orr	Campbell of Argyll, MacGregor
Parlane	MacFarlane
Paterson/ Patterson	MacLaren, Lamont, MacAulay
Patrick	Lamont
Paul	Cameron, Mackintosh, Mackay,
Peter	MacGregor
Philipson	MacDonell of Keppoch

Name	Clan(s)/Family & Tartan
Pringle	Pringle
Purcell	MacDonald (Clan Donald, North and South)
Quarrie	Macquarrie
Rae	MacRae
Ramsay	Ramsay
Rankin	Maclean of Coll
Rattray	Murray
Reid	Robertson of Strathloch
Reoch	Farquharson, MacDonald (Clan Donald, North and South)
Revie	MacDonald (Clan Donald, North and South)
Reynolds	Reynolds
Richardson	Buchanan
Ritchie	Mackintosh
Robb	MacFarlane
Robertson	Robertson
Robinson	Robinson

Name	Clan(s)/Family & Tartan	Name	Clan(s)/Family & Tartan
Syme	Fraser	Wallace	Wallace
Symon	Fraser	Wallis	Wallace
Taggart	Ross	Watson	Buchanan, Forbes, Watson
Tait	Tait	Watt	As above
Taylor	Cameron	Webster	MacFarlane
Thomas	Campbell of Argyll	Weir	Buchanan, Weir
Thomason	As above, also MacFarlane	Wemyss	MacDuff
Thompson	Campbell of Argyll	White	MacGregor, Lamont
Thomson	Campbell of Argyll, Thomson	Whyte	As above
Todd	As above	Williamson	Gunn, Mackay
Turnbull	Gordon	Wilson	Gunn, Wilson
Turner	Turnbull	Wood	Wood
Tweedie	Lamont	Wright	Macintyre
Ure	Fraser	Wylie/Wyllie	Gunn, MacFarlane
Urquhart	Campbell of Argyll	Young	Douglas, Young
Vass	Urquhart	Yuill	Buchanan
Walker	Munro, Ross		
	MacGregor, Stewart of Appin, Walker		